TRANSCENDING RACE IN AMERICA
BIOGRAPHIES OF BIRACIAL ACHIEVERS

Halle Berry

Beyoncé

David Blaine

Mariah Carey

Frederick Douglass

W. E. B. Du Bois

Salma Hayek

Derek Jeter

Alicia Keys

Soledad O'Brien

Rosa Parks

Prince

Booker T. Washington

HALLE BERRY

Academy Award–Winning Actress

Kerrily Sapet

Mason Crest Publishers

Produced by 21st Century Publishing and Communications, Inc.

MASON CREST PUBLISHERS INC.
370 Reed Road
Broomall, Pennsylvania 19008
(866) MCP-BOOK (toll free)
www.masoncrest.com

Printed in the United States of America.

First Printing

9 8 7 6 5 4 3 2 1

Library of Congress Cataloging-in-Publication Data

Sapet, Kerrily, 1972–
    Halle Berry / Kerrily Sapet.
        p. cm. — (Transcending race in America)
    Includes bibliographical references and index.
    ISBN 978-1-4222-1612-5 (hardback : alk. paper) — ISBN 978-1-4222-1626-2 (pbk.)
    1. Berry, Halle—Juvenile literature. 2. Motion picture actors and actresses—United States—Biography—Juvenile literature. 3. African American motion picture actors and actresses—Biography—Juvenile literature. I. Title.
PN2287.B4377S37 2010
791.4302'8092—dc22
[B]   2009022763

Table of Contents

" I HAVE BROTHERS, SISTERS, NIECES,
NEPHEWS, UNCLES, AND COUSINS,
OF EVERY RACE AND EVERY HUE,
SCATTERED ACROSS THREE CONTINENTS,
AND FOR AS LONG AS I LIVE,
I WILL NEVER FORGET THAT
IN NO OTHER COUNTRY ON EARTH
IS MY STORY EVEN POSSIBLE. "

" WE MAY HAVE DIFFERENT STORIES,
BUT WE HOLD COMMON HOPES. . . .
WE MAY NOT LOOK THE SAME
AND WE MAY NOT HAVE
COME FROM THE SAME PLACE,
BUT WE ALL WANT TO MOVE
IN THE SAME DIRECTION —
TOWARDS A BETTER FUTURE . . . "

— BARACK OBAMA, 44TH PRESIDENT
OF THE UNITED STATES OF AMERICA

1

AN HISTORIC NIGHT IN HOLLYWOOD

OSCAR NIGHT, 2002. FIVE NOMINATED actresses sparkled in glamorous dresses. Hundreds of stars and millions of TV viewers wondered which one would win the Oscar, or **Academy Award**, for Best Actress. The presenter opened the secret envelope. He announced, "The Oscar goes to . . . Halle Berry." She was the first African American to win for Best Actress in 73 years.

Stunned, Halle rose from her seat. Few people had expected her to win for her role in the movie *Monster's Ball*. She hadn't even prepared a speech. Tears streamed down her face as she thought of the **racism** African-American actresses had faced for years. When Halle accepted the gleaming gold Oscar statue she gasped,

Halle Berry looks stunning as she arrives at the 2002 Academy Awards. That evening was historic because Halle was the first African American to win the Oscar for Best Actress. She felt her award made it possible for women of color to get better movie roles in the future.

> **"**This moment is so much bigger than me. This moment is for Dorothy Dandridge, Lena Horne, Diahann Carroll. It's for the women that stand beside me, Jada Pinkett, Angela Bassett, Vivica Fox. And it's for every nameless, faceless woman of color that now has a chance because this door tonight has been opened. Thank you. I'm so honored.**"**

THE ICING ON THE CAKE

Film actors and actresses can win many different awards. The Oscar, awarded by the Academy of Motion Picture Arts and Sciences, is considered the most prestigious. Halle has won dozens of awards throughout her career, but she called her Oscar "the icing, the candles on the cake, the cherry on the sundae."

Halle has starred in 28 movies and numerous TV shows. She has appeared as a superhero, a drug addict, a movie star, a murderer, and many other characters. Halle has earned millions of dollars and achieved more than most actresses do in a lifetime. Her success is especially amazing considering the difficulties she had to overcome.

From an early age, Halle faced abuse and racism because she is biracial. Her mother is white and her father is African American. Most people view her as African American. Halle sometimes didn't receive roles in movies because of the color of her skin. She had to fight to be taken seriously as an actress. Directors often said she was too beautiful and glamorous to play difficult roles, like her character in *Monster's Ball*. Halle's mother encouraged her to dream. Halle said in her Oscar speech,

> **"**I want to thank my mom who has given me the strength to fight every single day, to be who I want to be and to give me the courage to dream, that this dream might be happening and possible for me.**"**

A DOUBLE WIN

For many years, African-American actors and actresses hadn't been recognized for their talent or given chances to play parts in

Halle cries as she gives her acceptance speech after winning the Oscar for her role in the film *Monster's Ball*. She thanked her mother, who through the years had always encouraged her to be the best she could be, even in the face of racial discrimination.

movies and on television. Although black actresses had occasionally been nominated for Best Actress, none had received the Oscar until Halle. That night she was part of a history-making duo.

Denzel Washington, an African American, won the Oscar for Best Actor for his role in the movie *Training Day*. It was the first

Halle and Best Actor winner Denzel Washington proudly pose with their Academy awards. Not only had Halle's win made history, but that night in 2002 also marked the first time Oscars had gone to African Americans for both Best Actress and Best Actor.

time African Americans had taken home Oscars for Best Actor and Best Actress in the same year. Backstage, Halle said,

❝I never thought this would be possible in my life-time. I hope we will start to be judged on our merits and our work. This moment, it's not really just about me, it's about so many people that went before me. It's about people who are fighting alongside me . . .❞

A Leading Man

To Denzel Washington, movies are magical. "Being an actor is about creating that magic," he once said. Famous for his acting skill, he has starred in more than 40 movies, playing everything from a boxer to a doctor.

Moviegoers love to watch Denzel on the big screen. In 2006 and 2007, they voted him America's Favorite Movie Star. He has received many awards for his performances. His 2002 Academy Award was his second. In 1989, he won for Best Supporting Actor. As of 2009, he has won more Oscars and received more nominations than any black actor in history.

Denzel Washington's roles often highlight African-American history. He has played slaves and leaders in the **civil rights movement**. He said, "I am very proud to be black, but black is not all I am. That's my cultural historical background, my genetic makeup, but it's not all of who I am."

That night, the Academy also honored the work of Sidney Poitier, a famous African-American actor who had broken racial barriers. In 1964, he became the first black man to earn an Academy Award for his lead role in the movie *Lilies of the Field*.

Halle and Denzel Washington's wins inspired many African-American actors and actresses. They hoped these Oscars marked a sign that attitudes in Hollywood were changing. For Halle, it also was a reward for many difficult years.

❝I always knew that I was going to do something extraordinary, because that's the way I grew up, always proving that I was good enough. I had to prove it to the world.❞

HALLE VS. WORLD

FIGHTS. SCREAMS. NAME CALLING. AS A young girl, Halle Berry dreamed of being a princess, living far from her father's abuse and the discrimination she faced for being biracial. The challenges in her life made her strong, though. She was determined to prove to the world that she could achieve great things.

Halle Maria Berry was born on August 14, 1966, in Cleveland, Ohio. Her mother, Judith, was white. Her father, Jerome, was African American. Although the civil rights movement was sweeping across the country, people often treated interracial families cruelly. Making matters worse, Jerome was an alcoholic. Halle often hid when her father hit her mother and older sister Heidi. He moved out when Halle was four. She said,

❝I come from humble, humble beginnings. One mother and two latchkey kids. We went without a

Halle looks confident and strong in spite of early challenges in her life. She coped with an abusive father, a single mother struggling to make ends meet, and racism because she was biracial. Halle could have given up in defeat, instead she was determined to achieve great things someday.

whole lot of things; we had the bare essentials, but for the most part we struggled. . . . So I can understand having big dreams and little money, and no way of knowing how you're gonna make 'em come true."

Halle takes a walk with her daughter, accompanied by her mother, Judith. When other children called Halle names because of the color of her skin, Judith told Halle she was special and beautiful. Halle realized her racial background did not have to affect how she felt about herself.

BLACK AND WHITE

Kids picked on Halle, calling her "zebra" and "Oreo." Her mother helped her understand. She told Halle she was beautiful and lucky to be different. Halle said,

> **"Every day of my life I have always been aware of the fact that I am biracial. [My mother] said that even though you are half black and half white, you will be discriminated against in this country as a black person. People will not know when they see you that you have a white mother unless you wear a sign on your forehead. . . . I realized that my sense of self and my sense of worth was not determined by the color of my skin or what ethnic group I chose to be a part of."**

Seeing Beyond Color

Halle Berry, Alicia Keys, Beyoncé, Tiger Woods, Barack Obama, and Mariah Carey are all biracial. These people illustrate the changing face of families in America. Many children have a blend of races, customs and heritages.

Only 40 years ago, many states prohibited interracial marriages. Today, an estimated 59 million married couples in America are interracial. Whites, African Americans, Asian Americans, and people of all different nationalities are marrying.

Although more people are accepting interracial marriages, discrimination still exists. Biracial families face challenges and racist attitudes. However, they are helping break down racial barriers. "When you have the 'other' in your own family, it's hard to think of them as 'other' anymore," said Michael Rosenfeld of Stanford University.

Halle longed for a father. When she was 10, Jerome returned. He hadn't changed though. Halle said, "It was the worst year of our lives. I'd been praying for my father, and when I got him I just wanted him to leave."

Halle's father moved out after one more year, and was never part of her life again. Halle threw herself into school, proving she was as smart and athletic as other kids. She was "Miss Everything," she said. She battled discrimination. She didn't get a role in the play *Romeo and Juliet.* "Juliet can't be black," someone said. The racism made Halle angry, and determined to succeed.

BEAUTY QUEEN

With light brown skin, dark hair, and sparkling eyes, Halle was beautiful. Soon after she graduated from high school, her boyfriend submitted her picture to a beauty **pageant**. Within a year, she was crowned Miss Teen Ohio and Miss Teen America. Next, she finished second at the Miss USA and third at the Miss World pageants.

Halle (9th from left wearing white pants), Miss Ohio USA, poses with other Miss USA contestants prior to their USO tour in 1986. Her beauty helped her reach the finals in several pageants and go on to successful modeling jobs. Halle was not satisfied, however, and was determined to try acting.

Soon Halle moved to Chicago, Illinois. She worked as a model. Bored with being a "human coat hanger," she took acting classes. She said,

"Everybody tried to make believe that [my beauty] was the best thing about me. Then I realized no, that's not the best thing about me, that could all be taken away tomorrow and I'd still have all the gifts that I have on the inside."

In 1989, Halle sent a videotape to talent manager Vince Cirrincione in New York City. Her acting impressed him. She "lit up the screen," he said. Three months later, Halle moved to New York, her heart set on acting.

THE FIRST BREAK

Halle began to **audition** for parts in TV shows. She soon landed a role on *Living Dolls*. One day while filming, Halle collapsed and was rushed to the hospital.

Halle learned she had **diabetes**. People who have diabetes need insulin to help their bodies turn the food they eat into energy. She would need to eat better, exercise, and give herself shots of insulin. Halle said, "I was scared to death."

Halle was sick, lonely, and out of work. *Living Dolls* had been cancelled. Halle refused to quit. She said,

"When you go through bad times, you find where your great capacity to learn is. And I've been through really bad times with my career and personal life. Behind all that are lessons that can make you stronger."

Soon, Halle landed a role on *Knots Landing*, a popular TV show. Her acting caught the attention of Spike Lee, a director looking to cast a new movie called *Jungle Fever*. Halle's career was about to be jumpstarted.

Chapter

3

A
Star
is Born

SPIKE LEE PLANNED TO CAST HALLE AS A pretty, sweet wife in *Jungle Fever*. After reading the **script**, though, she wanted to play Vivian, a drug addict. He said Halle was too beautiful for the tough part. Halle fought back, proving her talent. Over the next 10 years, her determination would win her awards and roles in 22 movies.

Jungle Fever's story involves drugs and interracial relationships. To prepare for her role, Halle and her co-star Samuel L. Jackson visited dangerous, drug-infested neighborhoods. She wore a bulletproof vest for protection. Halle also didn't bathe for two weeks, so she looked grimy as Vivian. The movie was a huge success at the box office. Halle said,

When Halle appeared in the Spike Lee film, *Jungle Fever*, her star potential was clear. She wanted the world to see that she could do more than just modeling, and she hid her natural beauty in her powerful role as a drug addict.

"I wanted, in a major way, to make a statement. To come out swinging and hopefully have people see me for something other than what was on my resumé at the time, which was modeling."

A Man Named Spike

Nearly 40 years ago, Shelton Jackson Lee's mother nicknamed her tough son Spike. Today, Spike Lee is an award-winning African-American filmmaker who doesn't back down. In his movies, he tackles important, but **controversial**, racial issues. He often explores the conflicts between white and African-American communities. His movies, such as *Jungle Fever*, *Do the Right Thing*, about racial tensions in New York City, and *Malcolm X*, about a civil rights leader, have sparked debate.

Spike's films have been nominated for and won several awards, including two Emmy Awards and an NAACP Image Award. His ability to write, direct, produce, and act is unusual. He also has written books, produced music videos, and directed commercials.

Spike's films prove that a black producer and an all-black cast can make millions at the box office. His work highlights the discrimination African Americans still face. He has inspired many African-American filmmakers and helped launch a black film revolution.

TAKING OFF

Halle's acting ability had caught people's attention. More movies quickly followed. In *The Last Boy Scout*, she played a football player's girlfriend. Next, she took the role of a waitress in *Strictly Business*. Another big break came with the movie *Boomerang*. In the audition, she played a woman breaking up with her boyfriend. Her performance impressed actor and director Eddie Murphy. He gave her the role on the spot, immediately sending home other actresses auditioning for the part.

Halle was working with big stars and becoming well known. She also was meeting influential people in the movie industry. Still, her race often determined whether she received roles in movies. Some people believed that casting an African-American actress changed the theme of a movie. Racism had never stopped Halle before. She even started experimenting with writing her own scripts. Halle told *USA Today*,

> **❝Black women need to put their energy into their own projects. Like Spike Lee, someone has got to be a pioneer and get it done, keep trying when doors are slammed in your face.❞**

Halle landed the lead role in the TV movie *Queen*. The movie told the sad story of Queen Haley, the daughter of a black slave woman and a white slave owner. Halle related to Queen as a biracial woman facing racism. She said, "Had I been born a hundred years ago . . . Queen's life could have been my life. And that was horrifying." Filming the movie was physically and emotionally tough. Halle spent hours each day having makeup applied to make her look old. She injured herself falling off a horse. She also was playing an abused woman. Still, Halle loved acting.

Halle plays Eddie Murphy's girlfriend in a scene from the movie *Boomerang*. Her acting was getting good reviews, and she was becoming well known in Hollywood. While she sometimes still faced discrimination, Halle was determined not to let that stop her from having a successful film career.

In the 1995 film *Losing Isaiah*, Halle plays a rehabilitated drug addict trying to get her child back from his white adoptive mother. Halle noted how important it is to teach children about their background and culture and praised her mother for preparing her for the racism she faced growing up.

PLAYING NEW ROLES

For several years, Halle had been involved in abusive relationships. She dated one man who hit her so hard she lost hearing in one ear. One boyfriend stole from her. Another stalked her. Now, a friend introduced her to David Justice, a baseball player with the Atlanta Braves. Popular, wealthy, and attractive, he also was an African American. The two quickly fell in love. Just a few months later, early in 1993, they married. They each continued their careers, keeping homes in California and Georgia to live near their work.

That year, Halle had roles in three movies. She had a part in *CB4*, a movie about rap music. She played a reporter in *Father Hood*, and a football player's tutor in *The Program*. Halle also won an NAACP Image Award for her work in *Queen*. The award honored the contributions she had made to the African-American community.

Halle kept working hard. She was receiving bigger roles and better reviews from movie critics. She took a role as a **villain** in the movie *The Flintstones*, based on an animated cartoon. The movie was a huge success, earning more than $100 million. Next, Halle co-starred in *Losing Isaiah*. She played a drug addict who abandoned her baby. A white woman, played by actress Jessica Lange, adopted him. Halle's character fought to get the baby back.

Halle's character believed white parents couldn't raise an African-American child well. In reality, because of her own childhood, Halle believed differently. She said,

> **❝I could imagine my mother being told she couldn't raise me because of the color of her skin. When you love a child, it doesn't matter what color your skin is. What matters is that a black child is taught about his history and culture and is prepared for the racism he'll face. . . . I know it can be done because my mother did it.❞**

Blazing New Trails

The 1915 film *Birth of a Nation* portrayed black people as evil. The movie was set just after the Civil War. Many white people, especially in the South, disagreed with the freedoms African Americans had been granted after the war. *Birth of a Nation* promoted discrimination. After seeing it, many white people joined racist groups. One of the most controversial films ever made, it launched protests across the nation.

The newly founded National Association for the Advancement of Colored People, or NAACP, led the fight. The group had been founded to advance the rights of black people. The NAACP fought against violence and discrimination against black people. It also worked to promote a more positive image for people of color on TV shows and in films.

In the 1960s, the group created the NAACP Image Awards, which honor the accomplishments of people of color in music, television, literature, and movies. They also recognize people who support these artists and provide more opportunities for minorities in the entertainment industry. The NAACP has honored Halle Berry's contributions to the African-American community with four Image Awards.

A REAL STAR

The year 1996 began well for Halle. She became the spokeswoman for Revlon, one of the world's largest cosmetics companies. She replaced model Cindy Crawford, long considered one of the most beautiful women in the world. Halle was the first African-American woman to represent the company in advertisements and commercials. "When I was growing up, it was hard to find images of black beauty. Things are changing and I want to be a part of it," she said. She was becoming an important role model for African-American and biracial women.

Halle starred in several more movies that year. She played herself in *Girl 6*, a teacher in *Race the Sun*, and a woman accused of murdering her husband in *The Rich Man's Wife*. Halle's biggest movie at that time was *Executive Decision*. She played a courageous flight attendant in a passenger plane overtaken by terrorists. Many people noted her skill and acting ability. One film critic wrote,

Halle plays a brave flight attendant in the 1996 film *Executive Decision*. As she appeared in more and more movies, critics continued to praise her acting. They said Halle was not only a beautiful star but a persuasive actress as well.

"Ms. Berry is the most gorgeous young actress in American films right now. . . . When a performer can look like a beauty queen and persuade an audience to follow her anywhere, she's a real star."

MARRIAGE TROUBLE

Halle's career was successful, but her marriage was crumbling. The couple had grown apart and spent little time together. Both unhappy, they soon divorced. Rumors about the two celebrities appeared in newspapers and magazines. Halle said she felt like "gum on the bottom of David's shoe." She even considered committing suicide. She told *People* magazine,

> **❝It was all about a relationship. My sense of worth was so low. I had to reprogram myself to see the good in me. Because someone didn't love me didn't mean I was unlovable. I promised myself I would never be a coward again.❞**

As a child, Halle had witnessed her parents' violent, broken marriage. She blamed her father. Now she tracked down Jerome Berry. Over the phone, Halle yelled at him. She told him how angry she was about his alcoholism and abuse and his abandoning the family. Her father apologized. Halle continued to struggle with depression, and was troubled by bad dreams.

PLAYING DOROTHY DANDRIDGE

Acting was Halle's medicine. She took a role as a dancer in the movie *B*A*P*S*, or Black American Princesses. Next, she played a murderer in the movie *Bulworth*, starring opposite big-name actor Warren Beatty. Halle's busy career helped her get back on track. Her personal life improved too when she began dating Eric Benét, a musician.

Halle decided to tackle a project she had longed to try. She became the **producer** of *Introducing Dorothy Dandridge*, an HBO movie, and she also took the lead role.

Dorothy Dandridge was a glamorous African-American actress and singing star in the 1950s. She refused to play maids or slaves, the only roles often given to African-American actresses at that time. Dorothy was the first African American nominated for an Oscar for Best Actress. Halle felt connected to Dorothy as an African-American actress who faced racism. She looked through boxes of Dorothy's letters and tried on a creamy blue evening gown of hers, which fit perfectly. While filming, Halle often felt like Dorothy's ghost was watching her.

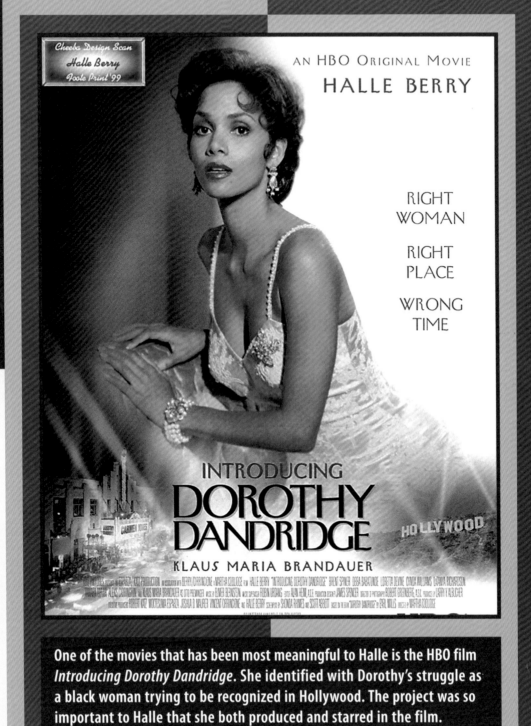

AN HBO ORIGINAL MOVIE

HALLE BERRY

RIGHT
WOMAN

RIGHT
PLACE

WRONG
TIME

INTRODUCING
**DOROTHY
DANDRIDGE**

KLAUS MARIA BRANDAUER

Cheeba Design Scan
Halle Berry
Foole Print '99

One of the movies that has been most meaningful to Halle is the HBO film *Introducing Dorothy Dandridge*. She identified with Dorothy's struggle as a black woman trying to be recognized in Hollywood. The project was so important to Halle that she both produced and starred in the film.

Halle's work on *Introducing Dorothy Dandridge* met with huge success. She received the prestigious Golden Globe Award for Best Actress in a TV movie. Winning a Golden Globe brought Halle more fame in the movie industry. At the awards ceremony she said,

"This movie was so personal: Dorothy's struggle was so much my own—to be an African-American actress in Hollywood. Tonight this said, 'I'm a part of this community and I've been accepted.'"

Halle celebrates winning her Golden Globe Award in 2000. After being named Best Actress in a TV Movie for *Introducing Dorothy Dandridge*, Halle also won Screen Actors Guild and NAACP Image awards. She finally felt she had been accepted by the film community.

Later that year, Halle won more awards for *Introducing Dorothy Dandridge.* She took home a Screen Actors Guild (SAG) Award and an NAACP Image Award. Halle was happy to have told Dorothy's important story because the actress had helped to break down racial barriers in Hollywood. Halle said, "Wherever Dorothy Dandridge is right now, she is standing tall and proud."

WEATHERING STORMS

In 2000, Halle was offered the role of Storm in the movie *X-Men.* The movie tells the story of people who develop superpowers and fight evil. Halle's power was controlling the weather. In the movie, she worked with other famous stars like Anna Paquin and Hugh Jackman. The movie was a huge hit, the biggest of Halle's career to date. She quickly signed on to do an *X-Men* sequel. Trouble soon followed.

Capes, Claws, and Cyclones

In recent years, moviegoers have seen superheroes like Spiderman, Batman, and the X-Men on the big screen. These movies are often based on comic books. The original X-Men comic, written by Stan Lee, appeared in 1963. The X-Men, or mutants, get their powers from unusual changes in their bodies. Storm, Halle's character, controls the weather, wielding lightning, snow, and cyclones. Some X-Men, like Wolverine and Cyclops, fight with powerful claws and laser beams. Others can read people's minds and walk through walls.

The X-Men fight against Magneto, a powerful enemy who can control metal. Magneto wants to control the world. They also fight against people who don't accept them because of their superpowers. The character of Storm was personal to Halle. She said,

"The mutants face many of the same obstacles that we do as African Americans. They're struggling to find equality within a society of nonmutants who fear them out of **ignorance**. Storm reminds everyone that, if anything is to change, we have to educate people out of their ignorance. That's the substance of who Storm is to me.**"**

Late one night, Halle drove through a red light and hit another car. She drove home, and Eric Benét took her to the hospital for the gash on her forehead. Leaving the scene of an accident is a

You can inherit it. You can be born with it. You can get it during pregnancy. You can develop it from the way you live. So is there any way to be safe from diabetes?

I am one of the 18 million Americans managing life with diabetes. Join me, Novo Nordisk and the Entertainment Industry Foundation in the fight to change the way this disease is treated, one person at a time.

To learn more, or to take an easy test for diabetes, ask your doctor. For more information visit www.DiabetesAware.com.

novo nordisk®

EIF
ENTERTAINMENT INDUSTRY FOUNDATION®

Halle is featured on a poster advertising diabetes awareness. She has helped others with this disease by working with the National Juvenile Diabetes Foundation. In addition, she has also supported charities that combat domestic violence and build playgrounds for children with disabilities.

crime. A judge ordered Halle to pay a fine and perform community service. She told reporters,

> **"I've developed into someone who takes responsibility for my choices. . . . It's easier not to dwell on mistakes when you own them and learn the lesson. When I realized I had the power to change, it was eye opening. It gave me a lot of hope."**

Despite Halle's difficulties, she helped others, too. She began to do volunteer work, supporting charities that were personally important to her. She donated time and money to the Jenesse Center, which helps families facing abuse, as Halle did as a child. Halle helped the National Juvenile Diabetes Foundation to raise awareness about diabetes. She had lived with the disease every day and wanted to help others. She also raised money for Shane's Inspiration, a charity that builds specialized playgrounds for children with disabilities.

Although Halle had faced ups and downs in her personal life and in her career, in the past 10 years she had made a name for herself in Hollywood. She had starred in 22 movies, both on the big screen and on TV. Halle also had proven that she was an actress with more than just beauty to offer. She could play tough characters. She also could take on roles in different types of movies ranging from comedies to dramas to thrillers. More fame and fortune was yet to come, and Halle was ready.

HALLE'S COMET

LIKE A SHOOTING STAR, HALLE BERRY WAS lighting up the big screen. Her acting skill delighted moviegoers and critics. People compared her to Halley's Comet, which streaks across the night sky every 76 years. Despite personal and career setbacks, in the coming years Halle would become world famous and make Hollywood history.

The year 2001 began happily for Halle. She and Eric Benét married in a quiet ceremony on a beach in California. Soon after their honeymoon, Halle adopted his daughter India. Despite being busy with her new marriage, Halle continued working hard. She played a government agent's assistant in the movie *Swordfish*. She starred with John Travolta and Hugh Jackman. Her talent impressed legendary actor John Travolta. He said,

Halle appears as Ginger Knowles in the film *Swordfish*. Her performance won her an NAACP Image Award for Outstanding Actress. Fellow actors also praised her ability to play difficult characters—even ones that audiences don't find likeable or attractive.

"She knows that the acting comes first and the looks come second. Looks are the icing on the cake. The cake is your ability to interpret a character."

Halle had long struggled to be seen as more than a pretty face. When someone slipped her the script to *Monster's Ball*, she saw an opportunity to prove herself and find true fame. The movie told the story of a poor African-American widow whose husband was executed for murder. The widow fell in love with the racist prison guard who helped end her husband's life. Big-name actors like Robert De Niro, Billy Bob Thornton, and Heath Ledger had roles

Halle and Billy Bob Thornton share a scene in the 2001 film *Monster's Ball*. She felt the role was her most challenging one to date. The movie was a huge hit, and Halle won an Oscar, an NAACP Image Award, and a Screen Actors Guild Award for her performance.

in the movie. Halle wanted the widow's part, but so did many other African-American actresses.

A SUPERSTAR

At first, director Marc Forster told Halle she was too glamorous for the role. Halle retorted, "Who are you to tell me that because I'm too pretty, I can't do this." Her toughness proved she had what the part needed. She said,

> **He almost didn't get to direct this film because he was new, and some people didn't believe that he could do it. And so I asked him, 'Please don't let me be a victim of the very thing that you yourself are fighting. Because you've never seen me do it, doesn't mean that I can't.' He took a chance.**

They filmed the movie in New Orleans in just 25 days. Although Halle was becoming a big star, she took time to encourage other actors on the set. When *Monster's Ball* hit the theaters, it became a huge success. Halle was nominated for an Academy Award for Best Actress, but few thought she would win. She faced tough competition. The night before the Oscars, talk show host Oprah Winfrey told Halle, "My heart is beating for you." Halle's win would be a huge personal achievement and an important milestone for African-American actresses.

On March 24, 2002, Halle won the Oscar for Best Actress. More awards followed, including an NAACP Image Award and a Screen Actors Guild Award. The African-American magazine *Essence* also honored her. At the ceremony, Halle said,

> **Although it was wonderful to stand in front of millions and millions of people on Oscar night, I cannot tell you how good it feels to be standing here in front of my own. . . . It's *Essence*. It's my people. It's my community. . . . I respect what they do, and to be a part of this illustrious group that they honor means a lot to me.**

And the Oscar Goes to . . .

Eighty-one years of Academy Award history. Four Oscars. Only three African-American actresses besides Halle have taken home Academy Awards, all three for Best Supporting Actress.

Hattie McDaniel was the first black person, male or female, to win an Oscar. In 1939, she won Best Supporting Actress for her role as a slave in *Gone with the Wind*. The first black person invited to the ceremony, she was required to sit at a separate table in the back. Fifty-one years later, Whoopi Goldberg became the second African-American woman to win Best Supporting Actress for her role in *Ghost*. In 2006, Jennifer Hudson won for her part in *Dreamgirls*.

Dorothy Dandridge made history as the first black woman nominated for an Oscar for Best Actress for her role in *Carmen Jones*. Although others have been nominated, only Halle has won for Best Actress. Her historic win inspired many other African-American actresses. In 2009, two African Americans, Viola Davis and Taraji Henson were both nominated for Best Supporting Actress. Although neither won, many hoped it was a sign that times were changing.

A WORLD CELEBRITY

Halle's Oscar win brought instant fame. She received constant media attention, being featured in newspapers, magazines, and advertisements around the world. On the Internet, fans buzzed about her personal life and career. She appeared on several popular TV shows. Some people disliked her success as an African American. One person hacked into her Web site and left racist messages. Halle didn't let the negative attitudes bother her. It only made her more determined to continue proving herself.

Next, Halle took on a role in a James Bond film. The popular movies tell stories about British secret agent James Bond. She played the part of Jinx, a beautiful spy, in *Die Another Day*. In the movie, she and James Bond, played by Pierce Brosnan, worked together to stop an evil plot. The movie made Halle famous from Iceland to Hong Kong.

Each Bond movie features a glamorous woman who plays the role opposite James Bond. They are often called the Bond girls. Halle said,

Halle is the newest Bond Girl in the 007 film *Die Another Day*. Her character, Jinx, is a beautiful, smart woman who teams up with James Bond, and Halle found the role empowering. Movie viewers all over the world flocked to see her on the big screen.

> **"When they first offered me the part, I thought what kind of Bond Girl could I be? You know, I really couldn't wrap my brain around it. Then when I read the script, I thought, 'Wow, the best kind.' I get to be equal to James Bond. How much fun will that be and how empowering will that be—not only for me as a woman and as an actress, but for other women."**

Brave, Bold, and Beautiful

Bond, James Bond. In every movie, the smooth spy called 007 introduces himself this way. The first James Bond movie, *Dr. No*, came out in 1962. Since then, there have been 21 more movies. Different men have played the British secret agent, from Sean Connery to Daniel Craig, who recently appeared in *Quantum of Solace*.

The movies share many similarities. James Bond fights evil plots to rule the world. He has cool spy gear, like jet packs and vanishing cars. He meets a different glamorous, beautiful woman in every film.

The Bond girls are sensational, tough, and intelligent. They often play villains or other secret agents. Halle was the first African-American Bond girl. As Jinx, she did everything from performing acrobatic stunts to wearing elegant evening gowns. Halle joined a list of other famous Bond girls, like Ursula Andress and Jane Seymour. Most women only appear in one movie, but each is memorable for her beauty.

UPS AND DOWNS

Halle began to star in even bigger movies, being offered more prestigious roles. In 2003, she starred in the movie *Gothika*, playing a psychologist accused of murdering her husband. Although Halle broke her arm on the set, she continued filming. Later that year, she again played Storm in the very popular sequel *X-Men 2*. By this time, she was the highest-paid black actress in Hollywood. She prepared for yet another superhero role in the movie *Catwoman*.

To play Catwoman, Halle adopted a cat, which she named Playdough. She studied how it moved. She would wear a leather suit and move like a cat in the movie. She also studied Capoeira, a type of fighting that combines dance, **martial arts**, and gymnastics.

Halle (right) appears in a scene from the 2003 movie *Gothika*. Suddenly she was the highest-paid actress in Hollywood. But along with the good came the bad: poor reviews for her role as Catwoman. Also, Halle's personal life was in turmoil with the end of her second marriage.

Although Halle prepared well, the movie flopped. One reviewer said watching the movie was "like claws on a chalkboard."

The movie received such poor reviews that Halle won a Golden Raspberry Award, or Razzie, for being the worst actress of the year. The winners of the insulting prize rarely attend the awards ceremony. However, Halle showed up in an elegant dress to claim her Razzie statue, poking fun at herself and the award. She joked about her failure. She told *People* magazine,

"When I was a kid, my mother told me that if you could not be a good loser, then there's no way you could be a good winner."

Halle stars as Janie in the TV movie *Their Eyes Were Watching God*. Again Halle showed audiences her command of a challenging part and her ability to be more than just a pretty face. Critics agreed, and she won Golden Globe and Emmy awards for her performance.

Halle was having other troubles. Although she and Eric Benét had only been married for a few years, their marriage was failing. Rumors suggested he had been dating other women. The couple tried to make their marriage work, but they couldn't overcome the problems. They divorced in 2005, another sad chapter in Halle's life.

FINDING HAPPINESS

Halle began working on another project. She was playing the part of Janie in *Their Eyes Were Watching God*, a made-for-TV movie. The story, by Zora Neale Hurston, told the tale of Janie, an African-American woman, who endured good and bad times in her marriages. In some ways, Halle resembled Janie. Both women married twice before finding true love. Halle said,

> **"I learned a lot, I gave a lot, and I was able to use so many experiences from my own life and sort of channel them through this character."**

More than 17 million people watched the movie. Critics were impressed. Halle won an Emmy for Outstanding Actress and a Golden Globe Award for Best Performance in a Television Movie. By 2005, she had won more than 20 awards for her acting. Her career was an amazing success.

Halle found personal satisfaction from helping others too. She continued working with the Barbara Davis Center for Childhood Diabetes, winning awards for her dedication and participation. She and other celebrities, such as Matt Damon and Usher, also helped raise money for the American Red Cross, which was collecting funds for victims of a tsunami, or devastating tidal wave, in Indonesia. Halle had overcome huge obstacles in her life. She wanted to help others do the same.

Chapter

5

~❀~

LOOKING TO THE FUTURE

HALLE BERRY WAS ON TOP OF THE WORLD.
After years of struggling, she had proven her ability as an actress. She had always shown she was talented, not just beautiful. Despite her tremendous success, she showed little sign of slowing down, often working on as many as eight projects at once.

In 2006, Halle played Storm in the third *X-Men* movie. Soon, people began talking about a fourth movie in the popular series. Halle's role as the storm-wielding superhero won her several awards, including a People's Choice Award for Favorite Female Action Star and a Black Movie Award for Best Actress.

Halle's numerous awards, including her Oscar, had inspired biracial children and many African-American actresses. She was always breaking down racial barriers. Halle told *Cosmopolitan* magazine,

Halle appears as Storm on a poster promoting *X-Men: The Last Stand*. Her role won her People's Choice and Black Movie awards, and again proved she could overcome any barrier to success. As she looked to the future, she was running full steam ahead.

" It feels really important to have won now that I have. Some kids have said, 'If you can be the first and beat the odds, then I can do whatever I want.' **"**

In 2005, Halle had attended a Versace fashion photo shoot. On the set, she met Gabriel Aubry, a model from Canada. The two became friends and started dating. After years of difficulty, Halle had found happiness and peace in her personal life. Despite the new relationship, she remained busy with work.

Halle sparkles with her star on the Hollywood Walk of Fame on April 3, 2007. The star was only one of her many honors that year, as she appeared in a critically acclaimed movie, received a BET Award, and was named one of *People* magazine's most beautiful people.

MORE AWARDS AND HONORS

In 2007, she made two more movies. In *Perfect Stranger*, she starred opposite actor Bruce Willis in a thriller. She played a woman searching for her friend's murderer. Next, Halle appeared in the movie *Things We Lost in the Fire* as a widow who helps her husband's troubled friend. Her performance was nominated for several awards. She won a BET Award for Best Actress. In addition, Halle was again named one of the 50 Most Beautiful People by *People* magazine. It was the 11th time she had made the list.

Many Hollywood movie stars dream of getting their name on the Hollywood Walk of Fame. The walk features more than 2,500 five-pointed stars embedded in the sidewalk. Each star honors an individual celebrity's contribution to entertainment. On April 2, 2007, Halle received a star on the Walk of Fame. She was star number 2,333. In front of a crowd of fans and friends, she tearfully accepted the great honor.

A Hollywood Legend

More than 2,500 stars sparkle on Hollywood's Walk of Fame. Each star features a celebrity's name. The stars represent the best performers in film, music, television, radio, and theater. Visitors love to stroll down the three-mile walk that runs along the famed Hollywood Boulevard and Vine Street. The Walk of Fame is one of the most visited spots in Hollywood.

The first eight stars were laid down in 1958, and included celebrities like Joanne Woodward and Burt Lancaster. Since then, each year more Hollywood legends are honored, from human celebrities to fictional characters. Cartoon characters like Mickey Mouse and the Simpsons have stars. One American president, Ronald Reagan, has a star. He was an actor before he became president.

More than 120 African Americans have received stars, like Halle. They include big names like musicians Louis Armstrong and Aretha Franklin, actress Dorothy Dandridge, and boxer Muhammad Ali. The Walk of Fame is truly a walk through Hollywood history.

EXCITING CHANGES

Halle and Gabriel Aubry had been dating for a few years. Despite their busy careers, they were very happy together. For many years, Halle had thought about becoming a mother. She had often played the role in movies, but she wanted to be a mother in her real life.

Soon, Halle announced she was going to have a baby. The couple was excited for the birth of their first child. On March 16, 2008, their daughter was born. They named her Nahla Ariela Aubry. The name *Nahla* means "loved one."

Halle had fulfilled another one of her life's dreams. She had long looked forward to being a parent. Her own mother had helped her through so many difficult times in her life. Halle wanted to teach her daughter some of the same lessons. She also wanted her to feel pride in her racial background. Halle told *InStyle* magazine,

> **"I want my kids to realize it's only through hard work that any success or real joy comes. It's not about money; it's the intangible rewards—having integrity and doing what you say you're going to do. My mom is that way."**

MAKING A DIFFERENCE

Halle remained busy after her daughter's birth. She wanted to make a difference in the world and worked with many charities and worthy causes. She helped prevent a national gas facility from being installed off the California coast. Several celebrities, including Pierce Brosnan, joined together and fought the facility that would cause air, noise, and water pollution. Next, she organized a golf tournament that would help raise money for the Jenesse Center. She also participated in a telethon to raise money for researching a cure for cancer, a serious and deadly disease affecting millions.

Halle decided to make a difference in another way, too. In 2008, Americans were getting ready to elect a new president. Halle strongly supported presidential candidate Barack Obama. She liked his beliefs and positions on important issues affecting the country. It was also inspiring to her that he was biracial, although people identified him as African American. Like Halle, he too had

Halle strolls with boyfriend Gabriel Aubry and daughter Nahla Ariela Aubry. Halle was thrilled to welcome her new baby in 2008 and hopes to teach her daughter the same life lessons and racial pride she learned from her own mother.

Halle wears a "Barack the Vote" T-shirt encouraging voting and promoting Obama for president. In 2008 Halle felt she could make a difference by supporting Obama, both because of his political views and because he was also biracial and had overcome racism to be elected to America's highest office.

risen above racism in his life. Americans had never elected an African-American president before.

Halle and other celebrities banded together to **campaign** for Barack Obama. She helped his cause by wearing Obama T-shirts, donating money, and calling voters and asking for their support. She told reporters,

> **"**I'll do whatever he says to do. I'll collect paper cups off the ground to make his pathway clear. . . . We are really going to need a president who has the ability to think big, and Barack Obama is that president.**"**

In November 2008, Halle and millions of Americans elected Barack Obama as their new president. She and several other stars again helped raise money to cover the costs of **inauguration** festivities in Washington D.C. in January. Barack Obama's success was a historic moment in the country. When Halle was born, few would have dreamed a black man would one day be president. People hoped his election would help change people's attitudes about discrimination.

Hopes and Dreams

When Barack Obama ran for U.S. president in 2008, many celebrities enthusiastically supported him. They liked his values and many ideas for the country. Movie, TV, and music stars hoped to help him get elected. Using their fame and fortune, they brought attention to his cause.

Halle and TV show host Oprah Winfrey were just two of many. Other stars like Robert De Niro, Usher, Chris Rock, and Kelly Hu, from *X-Men*, also helped. The famous Black Eyed Peas teamed up with others to make a pro-Obama video.

The stars donated money to help finance Barack Obama's presidential campaign and encouraged people to vote by holding telethons. They called people's homes, knocked on people's doors, gave many speeches, stuffed envelopes, and installed yard signs advertising Barack Obama.

When Barack Obama won the election, celebrities raised more money to help fund his inauguration. Many famous people attended Barack Obama's Neighborhood Inaugural Ball, a huge party honoring the new president. They helped celebrate the election of the country's first African-American president.

NEW PROJECTS

Like Barack Obama, Halle also inspired African Americans. In February 2009, she and Tyler Perry, an African-American producer and actor, hosted the NAACP Image Awards. They helped to honor the outstanding achievements of people of color in the arts. Halle stood as a shining example, as she had won four NAACP Image Awards. That same year, Halle served as a presenter at the Academy Awards.

Halle continued acting, working on many more movies and special projects. She began filming *Frankie and Alice*, playing a young woman with multiple personalities. She also began the movie *Nappily Ever After*, a project she worked on with biracial singer Alicia Keys. The movie explored ideas about beauty, relationships, and African-American culture. Although Halle had won numerous awards, she planned to keep making movies for many years. She said,

> **"I just don't want to go away. I haven't let the disappointments, missteps, or failures harden or jade me. Setbacks reenergize me. They make me realize that I have more work to do."**

Although busy with her extraordinary career and family, Halle didn't stop helping others. She continued to work with the Jenesse Center. She ran their Year of Giving Campaign, setting a goal of raising more than $2 million to help families suffering from abuse. To help raise money, she auctioned off a bracelet she wore in an advertisement for her new perfume, Halle, that was selling in stores.

Halle, like many other celebrities, also reached out to children affected by serious health problems. She worked with the Make-A-Wish Foundation. The charity helps grant wishes to many children suffering from life-threatening illnesses. Halle also served as the first celebrity ambassador for the Diabetes Aware Campaign. She hoped to help people face and deal with the disease she battled each day.

Halle and Tyler Perry host the 2009 NAACP Image Awards. That night she served as a good example of outstanding achievement because she had won four Image awards herself. But Halle isn't content to just receive awards. She happily keeps working on many movie projects and continues to support several charities.

A BRIGHT FUTURE

For 20 years, Halle Berry has lit up the big screen and entertained moviegoers. Her roles range from glamorous to tough and gritty. Halle's cast of characters includes superheroes, models, singers, spies, and drug addicts. Her list of movies is equally impressive, with roles in 29 movies and numerous made-for-TV movies. Halle's acting skill has won her the most prestigious awards in the movie industry and honors for her contributions to the African-American community.

Halle's success has been the result of early struggles and constant hard work. Her numerous movies and awards have showcased her powerful acting skills. As she has quietly overcome many obstacles caused by her biracial heritage, she continues to inspire others to look to the future and always follow their dreams.

Halle has worked hard to be the glamorous movie star she is today. As an African American she has struggled to prove her powerful acting abilities. Although she is well known for her beauty, she focuses on the person within. Despite her success, fame, and wealth, Halle lives her life remembering kindness towards others. She said,

"Beauty is not just physical. It's about what you stand for, how you live your life."

Halle's life has not always been easy. She grew up with an abusive father. For years, she faced difficulties in her relationships and marriages. Twice-divorced, Halle has now found happiness with Gabriel Aubry and their young daughter.

For years, Halle has faced discrimination as a biracial individual. As a famous star, she still encounters racism. These obstacles only make her stronger. Halle once told reporters,

"[My mother] taught me a lot about my history, where I came from, and how to maybe deal with racism. Don't get mad about it, don't get militant about it, but make quiet change, you know. Live a good life, and work hard at whatever I decide to do. And that's the best revenge, to succeed in this country where maybe people don't want to see us as a race succeed."

1966 Halle Maria Berry is born to Judith, a white woman, and Jerome, an African American, on August 14 in Cleveland, Ohio.

1970 Halle's father moves out.

1984 Graduates from high school.

Wins several beauty pageants.

1989 Lands a role on *Living Dolls*.

Is diagnosed with diabetes.

1991 Lands first major movie role in Spike Lee's *Jungle Fever*.

1993 Marries baseball player David Justice.

1994 Co-stars in *The Flintstones*.

1995 Wins an NAACP Image Award for her role in *Queen*.

1996 Becomes the first African-American spokeswoman for Revlon Cosmetics.

1997 Divorces David Justice.

1999 Stars in *Introducing Dorothy Dandridge*, a made-for-television movie.

2000 Plays the role of Storm in *X-Men*.

Wins Golden Globe and Emmy awards for her performance as Dorothy Dandridge.

2001 Co-stars in *Monster's Ball* and *Swordfish*.

Marries musician Eric Benet.

2002 Wins an Academy Award for *Monster's Ball*.

Becomes the first African-American Bond girl in *Die Another Day*.

Named the Make-A-Wish Celebrity Wish Granter of the Year.

Wins numerous other awards.

2003 Co-stars in *X-Men 2* and *Gothika*.

Wins an NAACP Image Award for her role in *Die Another Day*.

2004 Becomes the Celebrity Ambassador for the Diabetes Aware campaign.

2005 Divorces Eric Benet.

Stars in *Their Eyes Were Watching God*.

Helps raise money for tsunami relief efforts.

Meets and dates model Gabriel Aubry.

2006 Wins a Black Movie Award for *X-Men 3*.

2007 Receives a star on the Walk of Fame.

2008 Daughter Nahla Ariela is born.

Wins a BET Award for Best Actress.

Heads a fundraising campaign for the Jenesse Center.

2009 Presents at the Oscars and NAACP Image Awards.

Continues working on the movies *Frankie and Alice* and *Nappily Ever After*.

Filmography

1989	*Living Dolls* (TV)
1991	*Jungle Fever*
	The Last Boy Scout
	Strictly Business
	Knots Landing (TV)
1992	*Boomerang*
1993	*CB4*
	Father Hood
	The Program
	Queen (TV)
1994	*The Flintstones*
1995	*Losing Isaiah*
	Solomon and Sheba (TV)
1996	*Executive Decision*
	Girl 6
	Race the Sun
	The Rich Man's Wife
1997	*B*A*P*S*
1998	*Bulworth*
	Why Do Fools Fall in Love?
	The Wedding (TV)
1999	*Introducing Dorothy Dandridge* (TV)
2000	*X-Men*
2001	*Swordfish*
	Monster's Ball
2002	*Die Another Day*
2003	*X-Men 2*
	Gothika
2004	*Catwoman*
2005	*Robots*
	Their Eyes Were Watching God (TV)
	Lackawanna Blues (TV)

2006 *X-Men 3*

2007 *Perfect Stranger*
Things We Lost in the Fire

Selected Awards

1995 NAACP Image Award

2000 Black Reel
Emmy Award
Golden Globe
NAACP Image Award
Screen Actors Guild Award

2002 Academy Award
BET Award
Black Reel
Make-A-Wish Celebrity Wish Granter of the Year
NAACP Image Award
Screen Actors Guild Award

2003 NAACP Image Award

2004 BET Award
Golden Globe
Teen Choice Award

2005 Black Movie Award

2006 Black Movie Award

2007 People's Choice Award
Star on the Walk of Fame

2008 BET Award

Academy Award—a famous award, also called an Oscar, given by the Academy of Motion Picture Arts and Sciences each year to honor an outstanding actor, actress, or movie.

audition—a demonstration by a performer of his or her ability to play a part.

campaign—a series of events that help elect a person to political office.

civil rights movement—a period of protests in the 1950s and 1960s that helped end laws that treated African Americans unfairly and prevented them from having the same rights as white people.

controversial—an event or topic about which many people have strong, but different, opinions.

diabetes—a disease caused by the body's inability to use or produce insulin, a chemical that helps turn food into energy.

ignorance—a lack of knowledge or understanding.

inauguration—a formal ceremony that starts the leadership of a new president.

martial arts—skills, such as karate or judo, used for self-defense or fighting.

pageant—a show, performance, or beauty contest.

producer—a person who oversees the making of a movie or TV show.

racism—treating people unfairly because of the color of their skin.

script—the written version of a movie, television show, or play.

villain—an evil or wicked character.

Books

Banting, Erin. *Halle Berry*. New York: Weigl Publishers, 2005.

Hinds, Maurene J. *Halle Berry*. Broomall, PA: Mason Crest Publishers, 2009.

Kandel, Bethany. *Growing Up Biracial: Trevor's Story*. Minneapolis, MN: Lerner Publications, 1997.

Schuman, Michael A. *Halle Berry*. Berkeley Heights, NJ: Enslow Publishers, 2006.

Periodicals

Calio, Jim. "Halle's Moment." *Good Housekeeping* vol. 135, no. 2 (August 2002): p. 98.

Campbell, Bebe Moore. "Halle Berry: The Inside Story." *Essence* vol. 27, no. 27 (October 1996): p. 70.

Loring, Elaine. "Halle Berry." *Teen Tribute* vol. 7, no. 2 (Summer 2004): p. 21.

Seller, Andy. "Black Winners Make History, Honor Past." *USA Today* (March 25, 2002): p. D-2.

Web Sites

www.diabetes.org

The American Diabetes Association's site provides information about diabetes, including living with the disease, community programs, and nutrition and fitness tips.

www.imdb.com/name/nm0000932/bio

The Internet Movie Database's Halle Berry page features a detailed biography, recent events, and list of her filmography.

www.learner.org/interactives/cinema

Annenberg Media offers a look at movie making, with activities that explore the steps of creating a movie, from writing a script to acting to editing.

www.naacpimageawards.net

The NAACP Image Awards site tells more about these awards that honor outstanding men and women of color in the arts.

www.oscar.com

The official Web site of the Academy of Motion Picture Arts and Sciences features Oscar history, information about the awards, photos, nominees, and past winners.

PICTURE CREDITS

ABOUT THE AUTHOR

Kerrily Sapet is the author of numerous books for young adults. She lives in Chicago, Illinois, with her husband and son. While writing this book, she and her family enjoyed watching the *X-Men* movies and eating popcorn.